NICK JR The BACKYARDIGANS™

Surf That Wave!

adapted by Christine Ricci
based on the teleplay by Janice Burgess and McPaul Smith
illustrated by Susan Hall

SCHOLASTIC INC.
New York Toronto London Auckland Sydney
Mexico City New Delhi Hong Kong Buenos Aires

Hi! I am Pablo.

I am a surfer.

This is my surfboard.

I see a wave.

I paddle my surfboard.

I ride the wave!

Watch this!

I can jump!

I can spin!

I can do a flip!

Oops!

I do it all over again!
I love surfing!